Chapter 1

Introduction

Before jumping right into the definitions and the description of the machine I would like to brief to all of you what is radioactivity and why it is considered as a major problem in modern science. If we talk with respect to any layman language then we can define radioactivity as follows:

Radioactivity is a phenomena under which a given matter gains a lot of energy and in order to regain stability starts radiating that extra energy in the form of alpha, beta and gamma rays and during this process of radiation the matter will even tend to lose some mass of it making the radioactivity a major problem.

Now a question arises that why is it a problem? The answer is quite simple if a substance is showcasing radioactivity it will keep on radiating the rays as long as it gains stability, and talking of the time it may take to gain stability then it is a lot, so if we think to wait for the element to gain the needed stability and then start working on it will indeed be a really bad idea.

The radioactivity comes with two major problems:

1.) During this procedure the matter tends to lose its mass in term of radiations which is really bad news for us because if we want to travel through wormholes then we have to protect the main infrastructure of the shuttle. (Now some of you might be thinking how has the author linked the problem of radioactivity to travel through wormholes, Don't worry, this will be clear in the subsequent sections of the book)

2.) The second problem being we can't directly study radioactive substances as they keep on radiating various kinds of rays and if a human comes in direct contact with those rays then they will cause a lot of damage to the human body, this makes the study of the radioactive elements even difficult.

As usual a question may arise in all of your minds that is there any solutions to this problem, and as you all would not expect the answer is a big no, although we have started to use radioactive elements to our own advantage but the problem of radioactivity still persists and we humans haven't got any idea how to resolve this, making the problem of radioactivity to be taken up as a major issue in the real life.

Now we are equipped with the basic definitions of radioactivity which will help us to answer first question asked in the book that was why we need this machine and how will it help us in our quest to become an inter universal civilization

The answer to this question is hidden in the deep roots of the definition, as we again skim through the definition of radioactivity we can see that it occurs when an element gains a lot of energy and in order to become stable starts radiating that extra energy. Now in book 1 and book 2 of this series we had talked about the travel through wormholes and black holes, if we consider each and our concept deply then we can surely relate with the idea that despite creating the shuttle accurately and use the formulas described effectively the affect of the gravitation on us won't be less and under this influence of monstrous gravitational pull and the speed at which it will be moving it is quite evident that the shuttle will tend to gain a lot of energy and due to that the problem of radioactivity will surely affect the nature of the shuttle that we are travelling, so therefore we must try to prevent this from happening and the answer to this problem comes in the form of the machine that I am going to describe in this book.

So therefore this is the main reason that we are using this machine, our main target is to in actual prevent the shuttle form this major problem once it enters in the black holes vicinity because under the influence of the gravitational pull if it starts showcasing radioactivity then it will be a major problem for us.

Now let's move on to the main working of the machine, its components, its basic principles which will be discussed in the next chapter.

Chapter 2

The main machine

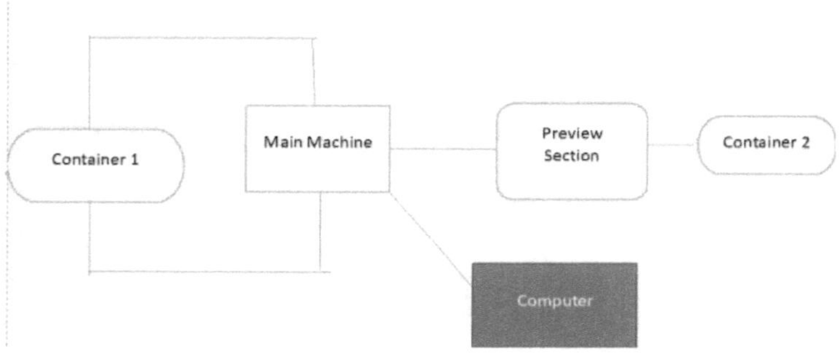

Now I would like to start describing the various materials and the matter included in the machine along with explaining why these parts were important and on how to increase the performance of the machine

1.) An input container: This will be the place where all the radioactive material will be kept. This will be the main part as the material which has to be recreated along with the information has to be kept here. So it will be a sort of an input area where the raw input in the form of radioactive matter will be placed. Now as this machine will be kept in the shuttle where in the starting the human subjects won't travel so the job of placing and collecting the needed matter will most probably be performed by the AI (Artificial Intelligence). So here again the AI will play a major role in helping the human kind in performing the experiments effectively and not posing any risk to the human life.

2.) A well laid system of pipes: Now when the shuttle enters the black hole the radioactivity will increase enormously in that case the matter that will be exposed to the machine in order to stop its radioactivity will be enormous, in that case we need a well laid system of transportation pipes within the machine so that the matter doesn't pile up leading to a serious damage to the machine. So that is why in the starting a pair of two pipes have been introduced, these pipes will collect all the material and bring t to the next step the main machine.

3.) The main part: This is the most important part of the radioactive machine; this part of the machine will convert the radioactive material back to its original form. Here first of all the atoms and the molecules that will be released due to radioactivity will be collected. Then it will be identified that form which matter the atoms have been collected. Now the information of each and every element is different from one other that is why two elements are different in nature if there information is different. But each and every element is made up of atoms so if the information for the elements is different so is that different for their constituent atoms. Once identified form which matter the atoms have been collected, the collected stuff will be bonded to give it shape of the original matter.

4.) The preview area: In this part the matter that has been finally created will be shown or will be available for preview so that any occur that has occurred can be identified. Once approved with the nature the matter will reach the final part of the machine

5.) The last and the final part: This part of the machine will be placed at the end and will mark the completion of the procedure of remaking the matter. The matter that has been approved will come to the collecting centre and can be collected. After this the matter that has been received can be tested and the conclusion will be that the nature of the material, it's physical and the chemical properties will resemble to the original element before it was exposed to such high energy that it started radiating its mass.

6.) The Computer: This is indeed again one of the most important parts of the machine. The main machine will only work if this device is working properly and effectively. The main work of this device is to identify which matter has been introduced to the machine on the basis of the information provided by the humans. For example if we are putting the Tiplurachyon element to the machine the prior information will be given to the machine. This computer will contain the resource bank where the information regarding the physical information of all the material which has been discovered by the humanity will be stored. This is the device which will indicate the machine on how to bond the atoms together to remake the matter.

As an example of how the above procedure will work we will take a situation under which a very well known matter will be made radioactive and exposed to the machine and with help of this I will explain the working of the machine.

The matter that will be used here will be the Diamond.

Diamond although being one of the hardest substances in the world tends to show radioactive nature.

Now let's see what happens if we expose the radioactive machine to the diamond:

1.) The diamond will be put in the input area; here the radioactive material that will get released will be transported with the help of the pipe system into the main machine where it will be further processed.
2.) Now all the matter that will reach the machine will be studied and the machine will separate each and every atom out of the emissions and will wait till it receives the signal from the computer after informing it that the atoms of carbon have been retrieved
3.) Now with the help of the information that has been already given to the computer it will identify that the atoms retrieved are of carbon
4.) Once the computer passes this signal to the main machine, the procedure on how to arrange the atoms will also be provided
5.) According to that procedure the machine will follow up the process and will arrange the atoms
6.) Once arranged they will reach the preview area
7.) Here the observer can see the final product easily, once approved it will be brought to the collection area where it can be collected and can be tested whether the product is fine in nature or not
8.) If during the preview phase the scientists find some mistake or disapproves the product then it will again come to the collecting area, here now

the scientist need to again make it radioactive and the process has to be followed up again till the time needed product is not received. This is a positive point in the favour of the machine as there are scopes of corrections and the product can easily be used. So above is the whole procedure of this machine will work. When built successfully it will help the humanity to regain any kind of lost matter and also somewhat stop radioactivity.

Now an important thing to discuss here is the principle on the basis of which the machine works. The important part pertaining to any kind of machine made upon physical concepts always corresponds to the principle on the basis of which the machine works:

The principle: The information is always preserved in physics and is a thing which cannot be destroyed by anything in the universe.

According to quantum mechanics the information the physical properties of matter are something which can never be destroyed in the universe. Even if the object containing that information can be destroyed but the information can never be destroyed. As an example when the needed technology will be formed if we burn a paper and collect each and every atom from the ash very carefully then we can club all the atoms together and attain the paper again. In the given example even if the object containing the information paper was destroyed by converting to ash then also the information remained intact and was arranged very carefully to get the original object back into the nature. So this is a really important principle on the basis of which the machine works.

Now let's discuss the obstacles and the advantages of this machine along with the solutions of the obstacles if any:

<u>The obstacles</u>:

1.) The preview section: Although the preview section seem to be a merit for the machine because it helps us to know the final appearance and structure of the product before collecting it thus making a room available to mend any mistakes that may occur in the process but the section comes in with some obstacles. The major obstacle being that the shuttle with the machine attached to it during the first journey won't include any human aid. In that case the AI that will be used can make mistakes and misjudge the structure of the final product and attaching the wrong product to the shuttle which can be harmful for the mission to reach its final destination. Now here a question arises that why I have used the term attached here, so we must note that significance of this term will be explained in the next section.

2.) The capacity of the machine: Each and every container in the world has a certain capacity; we can't out fill the container beyond that capacity. Same is true for our machine here too. The container in the starting of the machine has a capacity so the amount of radioactive

3.) matter that can be remade is limited. But once the shuttle is inside or along the innermost stable orbit of the black hole it will gain a lot of energy so a lot of parts will become radioactive and if majority of parts become radioactive it is important that all are put in the machine at the same time so that they can be reconstructed but the capacity will come in as an obstacle preventing the radioactivity of all sorts of matter at the same time which is a serious issue.

4.) The mass of the machine: The machine is ought to be heavy, with so many components getting attached to it we can easily say that the resulting space ship will be very heavy and a result of its mass it will surely increase the total mass of the body. Though again this will contribute in making the constituent speed that will be needed the object to be launched to be very small but the launching of a heavy massed vessel to high speeds with respect to it will be very difficult.

5.) The time it might take to reverse the radioactivity: Now here we end up having a machine which is so capable that it can reverse radioactivity and make an radioactive element back into a normal one and has a big scope to help the humanity further, But one of the things which is really important and a bit of concern for anyone using the machine is the time it might take for the procedure to complete. Now for the timing it's worth noting that the time that the machine will take at its initial built will comprise for about ten to fifteen minutes. Now this time is really a showcase of poor performance because once the shuttle is on for its travel to the black holes interior the matter will sure shortly become radioactive in a very short period of time. In that scenario if we suppose that once piece of the shuttle becomes radioactive in about 1 minute then in the time the machine will remove the radioactivity of one piece almost ten to fifteen pieces of the machine will be ready to get processed. So we have to keep in mind this thing and consequently we have to work to a point that the machine works very fast and very accurately and processes the material in less than a minute or if we work to make the technology very effective then we should aim for the working of the machine to process the material provided in less than a second. Once we attain this speed for the machine processing, then only will be the correct time to launch the shuttle into the cosmos.

6.) The Computer: The computer is although a very important and a very significant part of the machine but again it arrives with certain disadvantages. First of all it is important to note that for the procedure to take place the accurate information must be provided to the computer like the information regarding which matter is being placed to be processed and it is made up of which atoms. Without this information the machine won't work as the computer won't know which matter we have to make up and won't be able to signal the machine on how to arrange the atoms in it so that we get the needed product. Now the reason why it is again an obstacle comes with the view point that during the first travel there will be no human aid available that will give the accurate information to the computer, the AI being a machine is bound to make mistakes, in this scenario it is possible that any wrong information applied to the main computer will lead to wrong arrangement of the atoms and because of that any kind of absurd material can be created which won't be of our use can lead to the final debacle of the shuttle

Now let's talk about some of the advantages of the machine which make it very reliable to be used:

1.) **A room for mistake correction**: As on Earth when the machine will be tested for its accuracy being a machine there are chances that some mistakes may occur and in the first try we may not get the needed product. In that case we can again work out the experiment again by making the collected wrong material be radioactive and when we perform the procedure for the second time the probability for getting the desired results will be much more. This is one of the biggest advantage of the machine because in the long run there will always be a scope that any mistake won't be considered a failure and can be worked upon again to achieve the needed result. Now somebody would naturally ask that this will work as an advantage only when the machine is under the influence of the mankind, what if it again happens during the first launch when the humans will initially not be present, then what will the AI do if the product formed is wrong than it was desired. The answer to this question will be discussed when we will see the solutions of the obstacles of the machine

2.) **A complete solution to the problem of radioactivity**: Radioactivity is one of the major problems that troubles chemistry till date. Although now we have learnt how to use radioactivity to our own advantage but still the humanity is not able to uncover the secrets on how to control it. But the invention of this machine will be very advantageous to the humanity as now the humanity will be able to control the radioactivity and will be able to use the radioactive substances without any difficulty. So the invention of this machine will be an open testimony of the great leap the humanity will jump once it is discovered or invented.

3.) **The solution to the Moscrovium problem**: We will in moment talk about the Moscrovium problem that will be discussed in the given chapter. The concept of Moscrovium leads to an intense conflict between the scientists of United States and Bob lazar. Now the scientists of United States claimed that radioactivity was a characteristic of Moscrovium but on the other hand Bob Lazar claimed that it was a fuel that was used in the alien ships he had reverse engineered. But Bob lazar talked of another thing that was a special kind of radiator that he claimed was very special to the ship and also said that the rest of crew of scientists told him that once the humanity understood the working of that alien radiator they would excel in the field of science a lot. What if I say that both the US scientists and Bob Lazar are true, this can be concluded that aliens or the Extra terrestrial knew that the Moscrovium was radioactive but it was the only solution to the fuel that could help them to reach the speeds that we want to do now? So as a result they built a special kind of radiator as a result of which they could control the radioactivity of the element which had a similar working to that of the machine that I am suggesting to build. So actually the case was that the radiator present in the Area 51 as the claims are laid down by Bob Lazar that the ET knew that once they use wormholes to travel they would surely come face to face with the problem of radioactivity and as result they built a special kind of radiator that worked like the machine I am proposing and helped them to not only reach the higher speeds but control the radioactivity of Moscrovium. So same can be the case with the humans, we humans are struggling to find a fuel alternative. The Moscrovium can be a solution but the problem is the radioactivity but now here we can say that the problem of radioactivity can easily be solved with the help of the machine that I have suggested and I can say that the ET use that machine too. The Moscrovium problem will be explained later in much detail. For the time being it has been explained according to my theory but later when it will be explained it will be described according to the claims and the theories of other scientists from US and other influential people who purpose that the claims of the engineer Bob Lazar are true and then it will be explained that how a contrast can be created between both the ideas and later it will be discussed how the thoughts of US scientists and Bob lazar can be brought up to a compromise.

So now the all the points labelled above have been classified into obstacles and advantages, it might be observed that the obstacles are lot more than the advantages but still the advantages would convince any person to use this machine as the advantages overweigh the obstacles. The obstacles may hinder the procedure of the machine but the advantages are an open testimony to show that why a person must trust this machine and use it in the field of science.

If I have labelled the obstacles here it is very important that the solutions to those obstacles must be given out altogether. Because if we know the solutions to the obstacles it will be a lot easier for us to figure out on how not to let them create any kind of problem when the final experiments will be carried out.

Let's see the solution one by one of each and every obstacle and figure out if it correctly resolves the problem or create any other problem. And if the solution does create any problem then we will look out for its solution too.

1.) The preview section: Now it was stated that the preview section was an obstacle on the basis of the consequences of the machine being operated by the AI, the main concern was that on being operated by the AI it is liable that they will make mistakes and the wrong parts will be given out of the machine as a product, but we do not need to actually care about this problem. The main reason behind this is that once the part that is wrongly manufactured will be attached to the shuttle in no time it will again gain a lot of energy and will start showing radioactivity. So as a result again that part will be put in the machine to be repaired now the probability of any mistake by the machine is very low and if it again occurs then the part will again have to be put time and again into the machine so any mistakes at the initial point will be taken care of and the problem will be solved.

2.) The capacity of the machine: Now this problem is quite easy to solve, the main problem comes with the point that the parts of the shuttle that will be needed to put in the machine will be lot more than the capacity of the initial container of the machine, so the solution comes in the form that we can attach or deploy a lot of many of such machines with the main shuttle. The availability of a descent amount of machine will result in more capacity, means more parts will be repaired off radioactivity at the same time. But this would bring on a lot of problems. First the mass of the initial object will again increase due to a descent amount of machines being attached with the shuttle. Secondly the size of the shuttle will rise tremendously making it difficult to get fit in the main rocket via which it will be sent. So these new problems have to be taken into account and the solutions of them will be given after the discussion of the main problems. But it is quite evident that we must solve these new problems too because the difficulties they will pose will be quite serious.

3.) The mass of the machine: By discussing this problem we can figure out the solution of the new obstacles that were discussed in the capacity section. Now the major mass of the machine corresponds to the transportation pipe system as these pipes will be responsible in collecting the matter taking it to the main machine and the atoms that the matter will be split into will be collected by the pipes only. So for anything to qualify for the making of the machines transportation has to satisfy three conditions, first they must be light weight and secondly it must be non reactive and thirdly and most importantly it should not gain radioactivity once inside the black hole. The solution to this problem might appear to be uncanny, but the best solution to this problem is none other than plastic. Plastic has many positive points in favour of it which will easily prove that the use of plastic to make the machine transportation system will be very useful. Those positive points are:

a.) Despite being exposed to immense pressure and heat offered by the Earth at the bottom of the ocean the plastic never decomposes. If you dump plastic at the bottom of the ocean and the future human civilization will take it out let's say a thousand years later the plastic will remain intact and it will also not be felt that the plastic is a thousand years old.

b.) Some of the types of the plastic like PEEK and polyimide can offer a great resistance to the Gamma and the X rays. So it will be very useful to us as if the resistance to the gamma and the x ray are shown effectively that would mean that the machine will also be able to withstand the hostile conditions in the outer space

c.) Plastic is not at all reactive, this is very advantageous to us as we aim that the matter that we use to make the shuttles or any machine which goes into the outer space it must be not be reactive. So the plastic here fulfils our needs and as a result it is one of the most important positive points that favours that why we must use the transportation made up of pipes.

d.) The plastic is very cost effective, this point is very significant once where we are talking about the mission to be under budget then we can't really use any type of precious element like gold or silver, it will surely elevate the costs of manufacturing and launch which we surely want to avoid, as a result if we have something which can reduce the cost of the launch then why don't we use it, the usage of plastic will surely bring the cost of launch down and will ultimately help us

e.) The plastic is available in a very large amount and is spread all around the world, so therefore it will be very easy to arrange the large amount of plastic that will be needed for the project. This is also a plus point in the favour of the plastic because if we prefer to use other precious metals like gold or silver they have somewhat a lot of disadvantages. First of all the metals like gold or silver are very costly, secondly these metals are not present everywhere on the planet but there are certain places where these are found, this makes the collection of these metals very costly and they have to be mined and purified then transported to take the correct use of them. These processes involve a lot of labour and other costs which elevate the total cost altogether. Sometimes certain elements which may prove to be useful are found in other countries, so in order to mine them certain permissions have to be required which is wastage of both time and money. Speaking of plastic it is considered as a waste and most of the countries will be delighted to get rid of it and provide it free of cost to the main organization which will be very useful to us.

f.) This point is one of the most important points that will favour the usage of plastics over any other point that is listed above. This property is very useful in terms of the solution to the problem of the size of the number of machines that have to be included in the shuttle. The best way that we can find so that the number of machines can easily be added along with the main shuttle but in such a way that the size of the shuttle doesn't increase is to reduce the total size of each and every machine that will be included. So here the property of plastic that comes under use is that fact that the plastic can bend on being heated, the plastic shows this property only under the influence of a small amount of heat and is followed in everyday life by local carpenters and electricians. Now the main motive to highlight this property is that if the plastic can bend a consequence of that will be that we can coil out the main tube of plastic and make the initial pipes circular so that the surface area occupied by the machine reduces. When this will be done the size of the machine will automatically reduce as a result if which the total size of the shuttle won't increase and if the size of the shuttle won't increase our major problem will be solved.

So above are some of the important points that are in favour of plastic and explain and convince the reader that why one must use this cheap waste considered product to our own advantage. The use of plastic in the experiments will indeed come up with one more advantage that is the reduction of waste on the planet and with this humanity will surely become a prosperous civilization. Now let's follow up our quest of answering and finding the solutions to the obstacles that have been mentioned out for the radioactive machine.

4.) The time it might take to resolve any product's radioactivity: Now this problem is really important to be solved, this is because once the shuttle is in the outer space and enters a black hole the only thing which will occur each second is the shuttle gaining a lot of energy and a result of which it will soon become radioactive. In this case we require that the machine should follow up its procedure in matter of seconds and must prepare the desired product in no time possible. So it is very necessary to work out and a thing which needs to be resolved before it is the time for the shuttle to launch. The only solution which is best suited is that we accelerate the radioactive matter at very high speed in the pipes. The best way it can be done is described below:

What we can do is to accelerate the matter needed to be repaired from radioactive material at very high speed, in this case what will happen is that the object will gain more energy, this energy combined with its already gained energy will contribute to higher rates of radioactivity being showed by the matter, this higher rate of radioactivity means that at a fast rate the matter will be lost, now this matter will be collected faster as it is being released faster and then we must make the computer so effective that it will transmits signals rapidly, when the things will go on like this the matter will be prepared in no time and this all will reduce the problem of time when the main shuttle will be launched. So by following basic processes the machine can be made really effective and the problem of time will be resolved to the earliest.

5.) The Computer: Now the main problem with the computer was that AI that will be present during the first flight with the computer may feed the computer with wrong information regarding the matter that has been placed in the collecting center, if this blunder happens the computer the machine to arrange the atoms in a wrong way which will lead to the manufacture of wrong products and once those wrong objects will be attached to the shuttle, the shuttle can stop working and if that happens the shuttle will surely enter a stage where it will be spheggatified under the monstrous force of gravity that will be exerted by the black hole on the shuttle. A solution to it can be of the form where the part that although wrongly manufactured can again start behaving as radioactive and once that happens it will be easy to put that part back into the machine and again it will follow up the same procedure and under the influence of that what will happen is that the new product will surely be of better quality and useful. But to think like this is completely wrong till now the case where this thing was working was to think about the situation where the arrangement was correct and the information supplied to the computer was correct, only some errors occurred on the physical appearances like some dents scratches or any other physical trait but when the information was supplied correctly not chemical trait occurred, in this scenario we are considering about a chemical trait, For example we put in diamond and tell the computer about graphite so the final product that we will get will be graphite not diamond. So we cannot ignore this major blunder which will surely happen if the correct information is not supplied to the computer. So therefore we can't rely on the first solution where we will wait for the wrong product to gain get radioactive. It is important to understand that if the computer has the wrong information it will manufacture the products again and again with the same configuration there will be no change in the arrangement until some changes have been done in the settings of the computer. Thus the best solution for this is to use the human aid. But how? Before the first launch of the shuttle will be done the humans will surely check for any kind of error in the shuttle, if once no physical or chemical error will be found then only the launch will be initiated. So here what we can do is to give prior information to the machine regarding what the atoms are used to make the parts of the shuttle and what are their configuration, once this is done the AI just need to collect and deposit the products in the given channels, they don't have to do any changes with the computer. And thus the problem will be solved once and for all.

Now above are all the obstacles and the advantages of the machine. These will help to reader to get all the necessary information regarding the machine and how to use. The reader will know how to handle any problem that may occur in the functioning of the machine. Also these points will give a detailed account of the behaviour and the material used in the machine.

Now despite discussing these two points there are some points or questions still left unanswered, let's discuss them one by one by one:

1.) The problem regarding size of the machine: Although I have discussed the solution of this part earlier but this part still leaves us in a dilemma. A dilemma that questions the whole solution in this case. Now as a solution to this problem, I recommended the use of plastic which can be bent upon heating, in such a case the pipe instead of lying long will get coiled and the size of the machine will reduce. But in another set of solution where I talked about the problem regarding the time taken by the machine, I indicated that we must accelerate the input at high speeds in the pipe. But how can we accelerate something at very high speeds in a network of coiled tubes. The answer is quite simple the same way that we do in the LHC (Large Hadron Collider). In the LHC we first of all push atoms in the coiled pipes at high speeds and from there they are pushed into the main system. But now a new problem arises the components with which LHC plays are atoms or things smaller than the atomic size but here erupts the major problem due to which I was discussing this issue, the problem is that atoms can circulate in coiled tubes at high speed but what about a piece a whole structure big enough to be made to circulate in those pipes. Now the answer is simple, we can use the input container, to reduce the size only pipes were coiled but not the input and the output container. As it has been mentioned above we are only going to use plastic for the making of the transportation system, not the input and the output container, thus as a result the best thing we can do is that put the needed material in the input container and then accelerate it back and forth again and again and this thing will solve all the problems of the time taken by and the size of the machine.

2.) The type of plastic that we would use: Since the starting of this section about the radioactive machine I have covered many points about the machine, regarding the positive points and the obstacles of the machine. As a solution to many problems I suggested to use plastics. Plastic are of many types which are used in many ways in our daily life. Now the main question that arises is that which plastic to use? For this selection we have four categories to be fulfilled, first they must be light weight and secondly it must be non reactive and thirdly and most importantly it should not gain radioactivity once inside the black hole and the fourth and the last category that indicates that the plastic we are using must be unbreakable. Now the different types of plastics have different tensile strengths, some break easily while some don't. So in order to obtain the best results we must ponder upon the best plastic we can use for the process. There are a number of plastics which are suitable for the results. The list of plastics are ABS, polycarbonate, PPSU, UHMW and LDPE. Above is the list of certain amount of plastics which are the most suitable for the certain amount of plastics which are most suitable. Now these all can be used and will help in making the mission become successful.

3.) Why was the term attached used for the parts of the machine in the starting: This was mentioned in the initial points of the machine that we will attach the products manufactured by the machine to the shuttle. Now there is a natural urge to ask the question that why we are using the term attached in the solution. The answer to it is quite amazing. What will happen is that suppose we consider the condition that the shuttle is on its journey and has entered the black hole we wanted it to enter. Then it is obvious that the various parts will actually become radioactive. In that case the specific parts that will be radioactive will be provided as the input in the starting container. These parts will surely be attached to the shuttle at some point or the other. For example we take the case of a landing arm, suppose it gets radioactive as soon as the shuttle enters the black hole. So first it has to be removed and after that used as an input in the machine, when we will receive the final product out in the collection system, then we will have to re attach it to the shuttle, so this is the main reason why I used the term attached with the parts of the shuttle.

The last important thing that is left to be discussed is regarding what will be in the main machine and how will machine collect the atoms out of which the material was made up of? To discuss this and find its solution we have to think about one of the major advantages of the machine that is the radioactivity.

Radioactivity occurs when a certain substance gains a lot of energy and in order to become stable it loses the energy by radiating some of the mass in the form of constituent atoms into the environment. Here is the trick in the definition with the help of which the machine will automatically gain all the atoms that will be needed. I said that the radioactive matter release some of its mass in the form of radiation including the constituent atoms. So here as the matter will keep radiating mass the material will be collected in the form of atoms that will be released. So the machine will naturally gain the atoms that are needed for the procedure. Now a question arises that if we talk of some of the present day radioactive matter like uranium they take a very long time to get there all the mass present in them to be perished and uranium will be used as constituent element to make the shuttle, so won't this long time taken by uranium will be matter of concern for us. This is a right way to think because it is right that uranium takes a very long time to lose all its mass in the form of radiation but we must also note at the same time that uranium is a weak radioactive material this means that it shows radioactivity but to a very low rate. The rate of a radioactive substance depends on the energy it has gained. So material have a lot of gained energy thus they show radioactivity at a high rate. Now in this case where we are talking about the radioactivity of the substance once it enters the black hole it will be controlled by two factors first of which is the high energy gained due to the speed at which the shuttle will be accelerated and second is the high gravitational field of black hole. Now both of these factors will be acting in the same direction and when combined together they will provide a lot of energy to the shuttle. Due to this high energy the radioactivity will be shown at a much faster rate by the shuttle, due to this high rate the time will be compensated but to secure ourselves from any potential mistake that can occur we will follow up this in the procedure of the machine that we will accelerate the material at high speeds this will increase the energy of shuttle very much and due to this high increase in the energy of the shuttle the rate of radioactivity will increase enormously and once this happens nearly no time will be taken by the material to perish all of its mass in the form of radiations.

With this I conclude the machine section. This was one of the most important sections of the shuttle as it would only help us to reach the final destination. In the total process of explaining the machine I have started with giving the blue print of the machine, and then followed it with explaining that how the machine will be used what will be obstacles and how to get rid of them. Then I also labelled the advantages of the machine and answered some of the major questions that a reader might think of after reading the whole section. This ends our quest of understand the machine and how in literal it will work. The invention of this machine will be a major advancement for the humanity as the humanity will uncover some of the major secrets of science and will understand some of the concepts that were beyond our reach.

With this lets move on to make you all understand one of the facts that I have labeled above but haven't discussed it about much, and the fact is the problem of Moscrovium

Chapter 3

The Moscrovium Problem

Now some of you might be wondering that what is the moscrovium problem and why it has been included as a chapter in this book. Now speaking of moscrovium it is an element with atomic number 115 which has been included in the 7th period of the periodic table now most of you who know about the periodic table might have guessed that this particular element must be radioactive and might be thinking at the same time that okay if it is radioactive what is its use.

Now there is an interesting story behind it, it all started in 1989 when a man named Bob lazar came in front of the national TV and gave a detail analysis which was regarding the workings done at the mysterious Area 51 military installation in the United States. He claimed that he had worked as a reverse engineer there on the extra terrestrial UFO's and named an element which was used as a fuel in those ships and named that element moscrovium, the interesting fact that the moscrovium was not discovered by the scientists during the time Lazar was laying out his claims leading to a wide chaos amidst the USA where the people wanted to know more about Area 51 and its working there, after all of this massive conflict the moscrovium was later discovered in 2003 by the US scientists and the elements was named radioactive placing a strong argument against Lazar as radioactive element can't be used as a fuel. Now if Lazar was right then with the help of this machine we can use that element to our favor and if the ET's travel with the help of it then we can also travel using the same fuel, So this was the infamous moscrovium conflict that rose between Lazar and the USA scientists which I think will be resolved once this machine would be formulated.

Now with this I would like to conclude this book which I hope was helpful to all of you in understanding the nature of radioactive substances and in the end was a great trial to help to conquer the problem of radioactivity.

www.ingramcontent.com/pod-product-compliance
Lightning Source LLC
Chambersburg PA
CBHW021152130726

47988CB00004B/1576